Nutribullet Recipe Book

Smoothie Recipes For Detoxing, Weight Loss, And Vibrant Health

Introduction

I want to thank you and congratulate you for grabbing this book, *"Nutribullet Recipe Book - Smoothie Recipes For Detoxing, Weight Loss, And Vibrant Health"*

If you have just bought your very own Nutribullet, then chances are you are very excited about using it for the very first time. This is one machine you will certainly not regret purchasing.

The Nutribullet is mostly famous because of its ability to extract all the nutrients from the ingredients you are using to prepare your recipes, thus ensuring that you receive all the essential nutrients your body needs to function properly. The best thing about using the Nutribullet is its ability to break down even the toughest of ingredients, which means that you don't miss out on any important nutrients that would have otherwise gone unutilized.

In this book, you will learn:

- The nutritional benefits of smoothies made using a Nutribullet, and how it can improve your health

- How to make the most delicious and mouthwatering smoothies ever

- How to use your Nutribullet properly to make the best smoothies ever

I hope that with the help of this book, you'll have an easier time making all the smoothies you want without any problem

Thanks again for downloading this book, I hope you enjoy it!

Table of Contents

What Is A Nutribullet?

The Nutribullet is not like any other blender or juicer; actually, it is more of a nutrient extractor. The secret to this machine is its exclusive extractor technology that comes with a 600-watt motor and uses cyclonic action. This technology disintegrates and pulverizes the skins, seeds, and stems of your ingredients, which is where most of the nutrition is found.

Using Your Nutribullet

Extracting and milling using the Nutribullet

The two blades

The Nutribullet is designed with two blades – one milling blade that has a single blade only, and a regular Extractor blade with four sides. The purpose of the Milling blade is to mince dry ingredients into powders, while the extractor takes care of all the fruits and veggies. The blade you'll use will depend on whether you are preparing a powder or a drink.

The ingredients

Add your desired ingredients into the short or tall cup. The ingredients could be your favorite fruits and vegetables if you are looking to prepare a nutritious drink or hard ingredients such as seeds or nuts if you want to powder them up. The short cup can hold up to a maximum of eighteen ounces, while the tall cup can hold up to a max of twenty-four ounces. Avoid filling the cup past the maximum line.

- If your fruits or vegetables do not fit, chop them into quarters or halves.

- If you're making a drink, the consistency of your smoothie will be determined by how much liquid you use. Use less liquid if you like your drink chunkier. The liquid could be almond milk, juice, water, or any other liquid you prefer.

Place the blade you're using over the cup

When you are done filling your short or tall cup with your favorite ingredients, cap the cup using the milling blade or Extractor. Press down and spin, securing the blade in place until it is screwed to the cup. Process to achieve your desired consistency.

Loosen the stubborn ingredients

In some cases, ingredients may tend to stick to the cup, especially if they don't have enough liquid. You can loosen these ingredients by tapping or shaking the cup in order to mix everything together.

Save the drinks using the re-sealable lids

Each nutribullet is packed with 2 re-sealable lids, where you can keep your drink, in case you don't finish it. Secure them on the cup, and then place in the refrigerator to chill for up to two days.

Cleaning the Nutribullet

Cleaning the nutribullet is very simple. Just place any piece (except for the blade holders and power base) over the top shelf of your dishwasher or simply hand wash using warm soapy water, and then rinse.

Note: Never wash the blades of your nutribullet in the dishwasher. You can wash the cups in the dishwasher, but only on the top rack using the normal cycle (and NOT SANITIZE). In addition, you should never immerse the nutribullet blades and cups in boiling water as this will damage the gaskets and warp the plastic.

Stubborn cleanup

In case the ingredients dry inside your Nutribullet, you'll need to screw in the Milling blade and fill the cup with about two thirds warm soapy water. Place this assembly over the Nutribullet, and then power base for approximately twenty to thirty seconds. This will be enough to loosen the ingredients, after which you can apply a light scrub and you are done.

Cleaning the power base

The power base of your Nutribullet will scarcely get dirty, but this can happen if you fail to tighten the blades onto the cup securely, allowing the liquids to leak out and stain the activator buttons and base. Here is how you can clean it up:

*Unplug the power base from the socket first!

*Wipe down the outside and inside of your power base using a damp rag.

Note: Keep your hands and utensils away from the moving blade, and do not press the activator buttons using either your utensils or hands when the power base is still plugged in.

I am sure you are probably wondering why spend a lot of money buying a nutribullet when you can just buy a cheap and simple blender? Therefore, we will look at why a Nutribullet and not any other blender.

Advantages Of The Nutribullet Over Other Types Of Blenders

It is compact

Other types of blenders tend to be cumbersome, unwieldy, and too large to carry. On the other hand, the Nutribullet is small and lightweight, and it is very easy to clean, assemble, and store. In addition, it comes with 2 cup sizes (700 ml and 400 ml)

Easy to use

Unlike several other types of blenders, the Nutribullet does not have many pieces to be assembled, which makes it easier to clean up and prepare your smoothies. It is also very easy to use. All you have to do to start is to fill the cups up to the marked limits, secure the cap, put it in the blender device, and then push down and turn to start.

Breaks down the pulp easily making a smooth smoothie

You are probably aware that eating the pulp in juices is healthy for you. However, your kids may not agree with you, and they can be really picky; hence, you may opt for a juicer and miss out on the fiber and as you are aware many juicers tend to separate it completely by transferring it into a different jug to be disposed of or composted somewhere else. The Nutribullet addresses this issue by blending everything together for a nice smooth smoothie, making even the pickiest kid able to drink the smoothie.

High Speed

The high-speed blades and general shape of the Nutribullet cup makes it easier to blend the ingredients to a smooth consistency, which can be thin or thick depending on how much liquid you add. It can take about thirty seconds for the Nutribullet to attain a very smooth texture, but this will also depend on which fruits and vegetables you add, and whether or not you are using seeds and nuts.

Now that you know why you need a Nutribullet, let us look at why you need it to make smoothies. Why are smoothies good? What health benefits do smoothies offer?

Health Benefits Of Smoothies

Smoothies are one of the best ways to start your day. They take just a few minutes to prepare and clean up, and are a great place to start if you are looking to lose weight or get healthy. There are countless benefits associated with taking smoothies. Before we look at these, let us look at smoothie components:

Ingredient potential

Smoothies are a great source of nutrients and vitamins from a wide range of fruits and vegetables. You can make your cucumber, spinach, romaine lettuce, arugula, and watercress more appetizing by blending them with almond milk and blueberries. Smoothies also provide a great medium for incorporating nutritious foods into your diet, for instance omega 3 rich ground flaxseeds, hydrating coconut water, and protein dense chia seeds.

Vitamins and minerals

There are 6 general groups of fruits that are loaded with various minerals and vitamins. These are melons, drupes, pomes, berries, tropical, and citrus. Citrus fruits, like lemons, tangerine, oranges, and grapefruits are rich in vitamin C, folate, and potassium. Vitamin C boosts your immune system and manufactures collagen, which contributes to the framework of your body. Folate encourages healthy cells, while potassium helps stabilize your blood pressure. The berry class consists of grapes, raspberries, strawberries, cranberries, blackberries, and blueberries. They are packed with phytonutrients that help fight illness and certain antioxidants that reduce inflammation. In the tropical fruits category are the mangoes, bananas, pomegranates, coconut, avocado, pineapple, kiwi fruit, and papaya. Generally, these fruits contain manganese, folate, potassium, and vitamin C, all of which help keep your nerves, thyroid gland, blood sugar, and bones healthy. Common drupes include plums, peaches, apricots, and cherries. They provide vitamin C, potassium, and beta-carotene. Beta-carotene helps enhance the performance of your immune system and vision. Pomes fruits comprise pears and apples, which are excellent sources of potassium and vitamin C. The melon group includes casaba, honeydew, cantaloupe, and watermelon, which are all packed with vitamin C.

Fiber

Taking fruit smoothies can enable you to attain the recommended daily consumption of fiber – 38g for men and 25g for women. A single serving of fruit contains about 2 – 4 grams of fiber, with apples, pears, and blackberries having the most concentration of about 5 – 7 grams per serving.

The fiber in fruit is great for digestion, and can help lower your cholesterol and control your blood sugar.

If you are ready to jump on to the bandwagon, here are some of the most refreshing benefits of smoothies to motivate you.

Get your daily recommended intake of fruits & vegetables

It can be really challenging to consume the daily-recommended allowance of fruits and vegetables. Blending a few servings into a smoothie is quick and effortless, and can help ensure you provide your body with its daily nutritional needs.

Quick and simple

It takes only a few minutes to make your very own nutrient-dense smoothie, allowing you more time to do other things.

Kids love smoothies

If you have kid(s), then you probably know how hard it can be to get them to eat healthy foods. The good news is that most kids love the flavor of creamy smoothies that's sweetened naturally by a fruit or a good sweetener, such as stevia, maple syrup, or honey. You can even incorporate vegetables into your young one's smoothie, which they would otherwise not have eaten on their own.

Easier weight loss

Smoothies can provide you with all the minerals and vitamins your body needs, make you feel full and are low in calories. All these make losing weight easier.

Improved digestion

The Nutribullet will "chew" your food for you, and ease the workload on your digestive system to prevent indigestion and constipation. Incorporating some fiber can also help ensure flawless digestion.

Detox

There are thousands of toxins that we come into contact with daily that can lead to toxin overload. The ingredients you use in your smoothies, for instance kale and dandelion greens, can help detoxify your system and flush out toxic waste.

For Beauty

Think glowing skin, nails, and hair. Smoothies can provide your body with all the minerals and vitamins it needs to make your skin glow and healthier hair.

Meal flexibility

Smoothies can be taken at any time of the day, not just breakfast. As such, if you don't have time to make lunch, you can simply grab a smoothie, or prepare one in a jiffy.

Improve your immune system

Being sick is not your morning cup of coffee. Mixing the right ingredients in your smoothies can strengthen your immune system and reduce your risk of getting sick.

Reduces cravings

It is normal to crave sweets and other unhealthy foods occasionally. Fortunately, you can reduce these cravings, or even replace them with healthier alternatives in the form of smoothies.

How To Make The Most Out Of Your Smoothies

Drinking at least one healthy smoothie per day can really transform your health. Most people find leafy greens to be rather bland, and taking a green smoothie can help you add greens into your diet without having to chew or taste them. Here are some guidelines on how to drink your smoothies in order to get the most benefits:

- Prepare your smoothie in the morning, first thing after waking up, in the amount you usually take in a single day (1 or 2 quart liters). Drink one glass in the morning, and then store the rest in the fridge for later.

- Sip your smoothie slowly, savoring the taste and flavor in your mouth. You can also pour the smoothie into a lidded coffee mug, and carry it to your office. This will reduce its chances of spilling, while keeping it private at the same time.

- Do not include anything other than fruit, water, and greens into your smoothie. You can add seeds, nuts, supplements, oils, and other ingredients from time to time, but keep in mind that these items tend to slow the assimilation of smoothies into your digestive system, and can even cause gas and irritation.

- Drink the smoothie by itself. Do not eat anything else, not even a little cracker or a piece of candy, and do not take it as part of another meal. You can eat whatever you want about forty minutes before or after you are done with your smoothie. The purpose is to be able to obtain as much nutrients from your smoothie as possible.

- Keep starch vegetables such as green beans, corn, peas, okra, squash, pumpkin, eggplant, Brussels sprouts, cabbage, cauliflower, zucchini, broccoli stems, beets, and carrots to a minimum. Starchy vegetables do not mix well with fruit, and can even lead to indigestion.

- Limit the number of ingredients you add into a single smoothie. Try to stick to simple recipes in order to get the most nutritional benefits, and have an easier time on your digestive tract.

- Learn to make your smoothies sweet without including additional sugar. This will keep you always yearning for the next one. It can be hard to continue taking smoothies if they are not tasty.

- Always try to rotate the ingredients you use in your smoothies. For instance, almost all greens contain trivial concentrations of alkaloids. While these amounts cannot hurt you, and can even boost your immune system, eating too much for a long period of time without rotation can lead to undesirable symptoms of poisoning. Note, however, that it is not necessary to rotate the fruits in your smoothies. Most of the fruits in the market contain little to no alkaloids, and cannot produce toxic reactions like leafy greens.

Go for organic produce whenever you can. Organic food comes with several benefits, including the absence of toxic chemicals such as pesticides. What's more, organic fruits and vegetables are packed with superior nutrients that cannot compare to those of conventionally grown produce. In fact, consuming organic produce is the best way to nurture your body.

Nutribullet Smoothie Detox Recipes

Detoxification simply means cleansing your body of chemicals and pollutants, or getting rid of toxins from your body. Detoxing is a vital part of achieving and maintaining vibrant healthy, and it can be a great tool for losing weight.

On a daily basis, you are bombarded with toxins and chemicals from the air you breathe and the foods you take to the cosmetics you apply on your body, and several other things you interact with every day. While your body has the necessary systems to get rid of the toxins, we bombard with too much toxins, until you impair its ability to detoxify itself; hence, the need to help the body with detoxification.

A general rule of thumb is to eat foods that bind to and usher toxins out of your body, as well as those that promote your body's natural detoxification process. Nutribullet smoothies allow you to accomplish both of these purposes simultaneously.

Note: A typical detox diet entails consuming only the foods and liquids that help detox your body. This normally takes between several days, to a little more than a week. For better results, try incorporating small regular detox strategies to limit and eliminate toxins from your body. These may include eating organic foods, practicing dry skin brushing, drinking a lot of pure water, and exercising every day. Before looking at some detoxifying recipes, let us look at foods that have detoxifying properties so that you can know what to include in your smoothies if you want to detox.

Detoxifying Foods

Cilantro

This is a great herb for getting rid of heavy metals from your system. While the flavor may not be so appealing, its leaves contain certain compounds that can attach to heavy metals such as mercury and lead, and remove them from your body. If you find the taste too sour, try parsley instead, which is milder but has a similar effect on the body.

Limes and lemons

Limes and lemons are powerful citrus fruits that are loaded with vitamin C, a very strong antioxidant. These fruits will help maintain the alkaline and acid balance in your body, which will subsequently improve the process of detoxification.

Fennel

This delicious root vegetable has a subtle licorice flavor. It contains anti-inflammatory properties, and is a diuretic as well – that is, it has the ability to flush fluids out of your body. In addition, it stimulates an antioxidant in your liver known as glutathione, which has been shown to bind to and get rid of damaging free radicals.

Watermelon

This is a tasty and refreshing fruit that is very effective at detoxing, particularly helping in cleansing your kidneys and liver. It also contains a lot of water, which makes it an excellent hydrator.

Ginger

This brilliant smoothie additive supports digestion, and can help get rid of waste from your body by accelerating the speed with which foods pass through your digestive tract. Ginger also contains anti-inflammatory properties, and can help ease stomach upsets.

Dandelion greens

These may not be the most popular greens in the market, but they are the best at cleansing. They contain certain compounds that promote good kidney and liver function, and help these organs eliminate toxins from your body more effectively. In addition, dandelion greens possess a light laxative effect, and have been shown to work as a diuretic, further helping cleanse the body.

Kale

Kales are packed with chlorophyll and fiber, both of which promote the natural detoxification efforts of your body. Fiber combines with unwanted waste in your body, and helps flush them out of your system. Chlorophyll, on the other hand, helps to get rid of such toxins as heavy metals from your body. Kale is also rich in organosulfur, which can help prevent colon cancer.

In smoothies, kale tends to be rather bitter – so you can add sweet fruits like banana to help with this.

Watercress

This delicate green helps to oxygenate body tissues and improve circulation, which makes it an excellent cleanser. Increasing circulation can help your body flush out toxins more effectively.

An added advantage is that watercress can help improve the appearance of your skin.

Oatmeal

Oatmeal is packed with an array of benefits that are good for your health. It lowers cholesterol, reduces your risk of hypertension, is rich in antioxidants, stabilizes blood sugar, prevents diabetes, and boosts the immune system.

Arugula

You can also add this light green into your smoothie without altering its flavor. While arugula may have a mild spicy flavor, the taste is hardly noticeable when you incorporate it into a fruity, flavorful smoothie. This green has been shown to contain compounds that help accelerate detoxification, including sulforaphane and indole-3-carbinol.

Wheatgrass

Wheatgrass is immature wheat that is believed to possess powerful detoxifying properties.

Cranberries

Cranberries help cleanse the organs associated with the lymphatic system and detoxification, to get rid of plaque buildup and toxins.

Apples

Apples are an excellent way of adding flavor and sweetness to your smoothie without adding excess sugar. Apples are also loaded with pectin – a compound that has been proven to absorb toxins and help escort them out of your body.

Apples also contain another compound known as glucaric acid, which helps your body eliminate heavy metals and certain chemicals that resemble estrogen.

Pineapple

This is a tasty fruit that contains an enzyme known as bromelain, which helps cleanse your colon and improve your digestion. Just be mindful when combining pineapple with dairy products in your smoothie, as the fruit's high acid concentration can curdle the milk.

Yogurt

Yogurt is concentrated with probiotics, the bacteria needed by your digestive system in order to function properly. These microbes can help improve your digestion and boost your immune system as well. However, be sure to stick to plain yogurt, as flavored yogurts tend to contain plenty of added sugar. Use Greek yogurt if you are looking to incorporate more protein into your diet.

Spirulina and chlorella

These powerful green super foods can be very helpful in detoxing heavy metals from your body. They combine with heavy metals through a process known as chelation, and help usher them out of your body.

Beets

Beetroots are tasty vegetables that are commonly identified with their bright, purple-red color. Beets are often used in roasts, soups, and stews, but they can actually make great smoothies due to their natural sweetness. Beets are rich in certain compounds known as betalains, which contain anti-inflammatory properties, and have been proven to help repair cells, particularly where detoxification is mainly conducted, in your liver.

There are certain other foods that can help detox your body, but which may not be ideal to include in your smoothies. Try incorporating these foods into your meals to complement your smoothie diet: collard greens, broccoli, cabbage, fennel, artichoke, basil, sesame seeds, onions, and garlic. In the end, it all boils down to consuming a wide variety of healthy foods.

Cleansing detox smoothie (364 calories per serving)

Servings: 1

Ingredients

1 cup spinach

1/3 cup raspberries

½ medium avocado

1/3 cup cooked and cooled oats

8 fl oz Iced Green Tea

1/3 cup blueberries

1/3 cup blackberries

1/3 cup probiotic yogurt

1 fresh squeezed lemon

Directions

Mix all the ingredients into your nutribullet cup, and add the iced green tea up to the maximum fill line. Blend until it forms a smooth and consistent liquid.

Sweet kale smoothie (110 calories per serving)

Servings: 1

Ingredients

1 banana, sliced

2 tablespoons of chia seeds

1 cup kale

1 cup frozen grapes

Applejuice to fill line

Directions

Combine all the ingredients in your NutriBullet. Blend until smooth.

Citrusy oatmeal banana smoothie (333 calories per serving)

Servings: 1

Ingredients

½ teaspoon of orange rind, grated

1 tablespoon of flaxseed

½ cup oatmeal, cooked

½ medium banana, sliced

1 teaspoon of honey

½ cup Greek yogurt

2/3 cup of fresh orange juice

Almond milk to fill line

Directions

Combine all the ingredients in the cup of your NutriBullet, with the almond milk going last. Fill the almond milk up to the maximum fill line, and puree to your desired consistency.

The ingredients in this smoothie provide 21 percent DV of vitamin A, 51 percent DV of vitamin E, 149 percent DV of vitamin C, as well as omega 3 fatty acids. A combination of all these minerals and vitamins provides a very powerful antioxidant. In addition, oatmeal is a brilliant way to incorporate whole grains and fiber in your diet.

Ginger apple-carrot smoothie (112 calories per serving)

Servings: 1

Ingredients

1 medium carrot, sliced

1 tablespoon of lemon juice

¼ teaspoon of allspice

5 g ginger

1 medium apple, cored and sliced

½ teaspoon cinnamon

¼ teaspoon nutmeg

Water to fill line

Directions

Combine all the ingredients into your NutriBullet cup, with the water going last, and then puree the mixture to your desired consistency.

Green NutriBullet blast (164 calories per serving)

Servings: 2

Ingredients

1 medium firm apple, seeds removed & skin intact

1 (6-ounce) container of plain Greek yogurt

1 cup baby spinach leaves

4 thin slices of fresh lime, with skin

Skim Milk to the fill line

Directions

Combine all the ingredients in your NutriBullet cup, and puree until smooth.

While most green smoothies do not provide a lot of protein, this recipe is both high in proteins and greens. The apples provide sweetness and fiber, while the spinach is packed with vitamin A, vitamin C, and iron. The protein part is derived from the milk and Greek yogurt, but you can substitute milk with almond or soy milk, as desired. To add more protein, mix in a few unsalted almonds. This will increase your calorie count, but will keep you satiated.

Fruit NutriBlast (180 calories per serving)

Servings: 5

Ingredients

¼ cup mango chunks, frozen

3-4 orange slices

¼ cup pineapple chunks, frozen

4 baby carrots

½ apple, sliced and seeds removed

Caffeinated green tea

Directions

Prepare the green tea first, and then combine all the ingredients in your NutriBullet. Puree and serve!

Both Green tea and caffeine are excellent metabolism boosters. In fact, apart from containing literally zero calories, caffeinated green tea tends to increase the rate in which you burn calories.

Berry breakfast (112 calories per serving)

Servings: 2

Ingredients

¾ cup unsweetened almond milk, chilled

1 ½ tablespoons of honey

1 teaspoon of ground flaxseed

1 cup frozen unsweetened raspberries

¼ cup of frozen pitted unsweetened raspberries or cherries

2 teaspoons of fresh ginger, finely grated

1-2 teaspoons of fresh lemon juice

Directions

Combine all the ingredients in your NutriBullet, and blend until smooth. Serve in two chilled glasses.

The ginger in this recipe enhances digestion, while the berries stimulate detoxifying enzymes.

The super green (160 calories per serving)

Servings: 2

Ingredients

1¼ cups frozen mango, cubed

1 cup orange or tangerine juice

¼ cup chopped fresh mint

1¼ cups chopped kale leaves

2 celery ribs, chopped

¼ cup flat-leaf parsley, chopped

Directions

Combine all the ingredients in a NutriBullet, and blend until smooth. Serve in two chilled glasses

The bright green color in this recipe is due to the parsley and celery, which are diuretics that are great for getting rid of toxins from your body. The super-foods mango and kale provide the necessary nutrition for enhancing your cleanse.

Coconut and watermelon shake (109 calories per serving)

Servings: 1

Ingredients

1 medium pear, cored and sliced

1 cup watermelon, cubed

Coconut water to max line

Directions

Combine the coconut water, pear, and watermelon in your NutriBullet, and process until smooth, about ten to twelve seconds. Serve in a glass, and garnish with pear or watermelon, if desired.

Watermelon and mango shake (86 calories per serving)

Servings: 1

Ingredients

½ cup mango, cubed

½ cup watermelon, cubed

¼ cup fennel bulb, shredded

Water to max line

Directions

Combine the fennel, mango, watermelon, and water in your NutriBullet, and process until smooth. Serve and garnish with a slice of mango or watermelon, if desired.

The ingredients in this recipe are anti-cancer that can prevent cell damage and inhibit the development of cancer.

Grape and parsley beet juice (89 calories per serving)

Servings: 1

Ingredients

1 medium beet root, sliced

¼ cup of parsley, flat leaf

1 cup of seedless grapes

Water to max line

Directions

Combine the grapes, beet root, parsley, and water in a NutriBullet, and puree for ten to twelve seconds, or until smooth. Serve into a glass, and garnish with parsley or beet root, if desired.

The ingredients in this recipe (grapes, beetroot, and parsley), are potent antioxidants that can help prevent the effects of free radicals, which can lead to cancer.

Lime juice and honeydew smoothie (96 calories per serving)

Servings: 1

Ingredients

½ medium green capsicum, deseeded and sliced

1 cup honeydew melon, cubed

1 tablespoon of lime juice

Coconut water to max line

Directions

Combine the coconut water, lime juice, capsicum, and honeydew melon in a NutriBullet, and process until smooth, about twelve seconds. Serve in a glass, and garnish with lime or honeydew melon, if desired.

Cabbage and kiwi smoothie (82 calories per serving)

Servings: 1

Ingredients

½ cup cabbage, shredded

1 medium kiwi fruit, sliced

2 tablespoons of lime juice

Coconut water to max line

Directions

Combine the coconut water, lime juice, cabbage, and kiwi fruit in a NutriBullet, and process until smooth, about ten seconds. Serve in a glass, garnished with a slice of lime or kiwi, if desired.

This is a great combination of fruits and vegetables (lime juice, coconut water, fruit and cabbage) that are packed with antioxidants and nutrients that can help counter cancer and other similar degenerative diseases.

Cleansing detox blast (233 calories per serving)

Servings: 1

Ingredients

1 handful purple cabbage

1 carrot

½ apple

1 handful dandelion greens

½ beet

1 lemon, peeled

Water to max line

Directions

Combine all the ingredients in the NutriBullet, and process until smooth.

Leafy green vegetables are very efficient at cleansing the liver, which is why it is always advisable to eat more greens while detoxing. Apple, on the other hand, is a great source of vitamins and fiber, while lemon helps break foods down for easier digestion.

Banana Coffee smoothie

Servings: 1

Ingredients

¼ cup coconut milk

2-3 tablespoons coconut flakes

2 bananas

½ cup coffee, cold or room temperature

Directions

Combine everything in your NutriBullet and process until smooth.

This diary free, vegan, gluten free recipe contains some coconut milk, bananas, and coffee, which makes it very delicious and nutritious. The bananas are packed with pectin and potassium, and are great for strengthening your nervous system. Coffee, on the other hand, will help boost your energy levels and prevent constipation. Adding coconut milk will also provide your daily iron requirement.

Antioxidant smoothie

Servings: 1 .

Ingredients

½ banana

1 teaspoon of goji berries

1 handful of almonds

1 cup of coffee

1 tablespoon of cacao

1 teaspoon of chia seeds

1 scoop of protein powder

Directions

Mix all the ingredients in the Nutribullet, and blend until smooth. Serve in a glass, and enjoy!

Cacao provides a strong, delicious taste, and is also packed with antioxidants. The banana in this recipe will deliver deliciousness and add sugar, while goji berries are potent antioxidants that can help keep you young too. Almonds, on the other hand, are packed with vitamin E that will go a long way towards fighting off free radicals that can lead to cancer, as well as helping with kidney stones and constipation. Adding chia seeds will help balance your blood sugar levels and provide you with healthy proteins, while protein powder will help maintain your body weight and accelerate body recovery.

Chocolate mint veggie smoothie

Servings; 2

Ingredients

1 scoop of chocolate protein powder

1 tablespoon of cacao nibs or dark chocolate chips

1 cup unsweetened almond milk

Stevia to taste

½ avocado, pit & skin removed

1 drop of mint extractor ¼ cup of fresh mint

2 heaping cups of organic spinach

1 cup of filtered water

Ice (optional)

Directions

Combine all ingredients in your nutribullet and blend until smooth.

This smoothie combines chocolate and veggies to provide you with a sweet, healthy, and green smoothie. The avocado will provide you with healthy fats, while the almond milk is packed with protein. The addition of chocolate protein powder will enhance the flavor and protein content. The dark chocolate, on the other hand, is nutritious and can prevent the oxidation of good cholesterol, regulate bad cholesterol levels, and lower your blood pressure. You can also add ice to chill, and stevia to sweeten the smoothie.

Strawberry and yogurt smoothie

Servings: 1

Ingredients

1 banana

10 strawberries

1 cup of yogurt

Directions

Combine everything in the NutriBullet cup, and blend until smooth. Serve and enjoy!

This recipe is the best way to switch from unhealthy snacking, if you are guilty as charged! Strawberries are excellent for weight loss, low in calories, and high in fiber. Yogurt is a healthy snack alternative because it is rich in protein and promotes a healthy immune system. Bananas, on the other hand, are packed with potassium and fiber – the former will help improve your blood pressure, while the latter will improve digestion.

Vitamin C boost smoothie

Servings: 1

Ingredients

1 orange

½ cup of water

1 handful of pineapple cubes

1 apple, cored

Directions

Put all the ingredients in the NutriBullet, and process until smooth.

Vitamin C is a very strong antioxidant that is usually recommended because of its effectiveness against free radicals. In addition, vitamin C creates collagen, which plays a major role in enhancing the skin, bones, and joints. It also helps to promote the activities of white blood cells within your immune system, which can help prevent the development of cancer. Oranges are very rich in vitamin C, as well as citrus limonoids, which can help prevent kidney diseases (most notably kidney stones), and lower your cholesterol levels. The pineapples are also packed with vitamin C and antioxidants, which will boost your immune system and help eradicate free radicals from your immune system. Pineapples are also packed with an enzyme known as bromelain, which has been proven to enhance the digestive system.

eberry detox smoothie

Servings: 1

Ingredients

1 handful blueberries

1 handful raspberries

1 handful pineapples

1 handful blackberries

½ a cup of water

Directions

Combine all the ingredients in your NutriBullet, and blend until smooth.

This smoothie recipe is a great way to incorporate fruits and veggies into your diet and boost your immune system. The pineapples and berries here will provide you with a rich content of antioxidants and vitamin C, which are great for detoxing and boosting your vitamin intake. Pineapples are also great for your digestive system due to their bromelain content, which helps in digestion. In addition, pineapples are rich in vitamin C, which can enhance your bones and skin, as well as manganese, which secretes the enzymes for energy. The addition of raspberries will help boost your immune system, increase metabolism, and improve your digestion. Raspberries have been shown to contain high levels of antioxidants, which are very powerful against the effects of free radicals that can lead to cancer.

Skin detox smoothie

Servings: 1

Ingredients

1 mango

2 bananas

½ cup of almond milk

Directions

Combine all the ingredients in your NutriBullet, and process until smooth. Serve and enjoy!

This smoothie is made up of a few ingredients – almond milk, mango, and bananas, which makes this recipe delicious and simple to make. Apart from their sweet taste, mangoes are packed with several different nutrients, including vitamin A and vitamin C, which are very effective at reducing spots and wrinkles, and potassium, which is great for the digestive system. Bananas are rich in potassium and fiber, which are great for improving your blood pressure and enhancing your digestive system respectively. In addition, bananas are great for enhancing the taste and flavor of the smoothie, especially if it does not have a great aroma. Almond milk will help thicken your drink as well.

Belly friendly smoothie

Servings: 1

Ingredients

1 handful blueberries

1 handful blackberries

1 handful strawberries

1 handful raspberries

½ cup of water

Directions

Combine all the ingredients in your NutriBullet, and puree until smooth.

This is one of the best smoothie recipes for flattening your tummy the healthy way. It is packed with summer berries, and is low on calorie and high in nutrients. The blend of strawberries, raspberries, blackberries, and blueberries provides a sour but healthy combination, which will help with your digestion. Blackberries are packed with antibacterial properties and antioxidants, which are very helpful at fighting off free radicals. They are also rich in fiber, which will enhance your digestive system and flatten your belly in the long run. Consuming fiber rich fruits will go a long way towards helping you lose weight.

Nutribullet Smoothies For Weight Loss

Smoothies are amazing when it comes to helping you lose weight. This is because healthy smoothies are high in fiber, vitamins, minerals, and other healthy nutrients. In addition, they are low in calorie; thus, making them perfect for weight loss. For instance, a homemade v8 smoothie contains about one pound of vegetables, and is about 150 calories. You drink one of this, and you'll be full for hours. Even though it is more than five hundred calories less than a typical meal, it leaves you feeling satisfied like a full meal.

Following that logic, if you can be able to substitute one meal with such a satisfying smoothie per day, you can be able to lose about one pound per week. Smoothies are just a very simplified way of getting fuller with fewer calories. Before we look at some weight loss smoothies, it is important to understand what makes a good weight loss smoothie.

Characteristics Of A Good Weight Loss Smoothie

- It should be high volume (at least 16 ounces)

- It should be low calorie (ideally, not more than 200) but thick

- It should be comprised mainly of nutrient dense, low calorie, high volume ingredients

- It should be high in fiber and low in sugar

- It should taste decent

Note: Smoothies that are packed with tropical fruits (for example mango, pineapple, and so on), while may be delicious and nutrient packed – they can be easy to binge on if you are not careful. Keep in mind that losing weight does not matter whether your diet is "clean" or not. If you are taking too many calories, you'll not lose weight, regardless of where their source is. A good rule of thumb is to aim for smoothies that are between 100 and 200 calories.

The Importance Of Making Thick Smoothies And How to Make Thick Smoothies

The first rule of making smoothies, as far as weight loss is concerned, is to make it thick. As mentioned previously, you need to cut back on your calories, when you are looking to lose weight. As such, even though you are eating less, you need to ensure that you don't feel hungry all the time. Otherwise, you'll end up giving in to your hunger, and start looking for the nearest junk food to take.

Amazingly, you don't have to take my word for it. A study conducted in 2012 and published in a journal known as Flavour showed that thick smoothies could leave you feeling satisfied and full for longer as compared to thinner drinks with the same amount of calories. Scientists took 2 yogurt based smoothies with a similar amount of calories and added a thickener to one of them – tara gum. The results revealed that those who took the thicker drink felt twice as satisfied as those who took the thinner drink.

In short, taking thicker smoothies allows you to cut back on your calorie intake while still keeping you satisfied and full.

However, in any case, since thickness is relative, everyone will have a different opinion when it comes to how thick or thin a smoothie is.

Ingredients you can use to thicken your smoothie

Chia seeds

This is a great option if you are looking to thicken your smoothie. Soaking chia seeds in liquid will turn them into a gel like substance, subsequently retaining approximately 8 to 9 times their original weight and swelling significantly. However, this thickness takes about twenty minutes to become fully active. As such, if you take your smoothie right after you make it, it'll have the same thinness or thickness as usual and then swell up in the stomach to leave you feeling satisfied for hours.

Presoak your chia seeds in a couple tablespoons of water about twenty minutes before preparing your smoothie. If you are normally pressed for time, prepare your own gel beforehand, and then add one or two tablespoons into your smoothie when you need to.

Making the chia gel

Pour two cups of water into a glass jar, and add one third cup of chia seeds to soak. Secure with a tight fitting lid. You can also add one more cup of water if you are looking for a thinner gel. Shake and put in the fridge for up to two weeks.

Chia seeds are extremely healthy, apart from the fact that they are believed to have been the main source of survival for Aztec warriors some time back, with 1 tablespoon said to have been enough to sustain one person for twenty-four hours. Chia seeds are packed with calcium, antioxidants, fiber, protein, and omega three fatty acids. In fact, they have such a high concentration of antioxidants (more than any whole food, even blueberries) that they have a significantly long lifespan, and can stay for very long without becoming rancid.

Linseeds/flaxseeds

Flaxseeds, like the chia seeds, are often classified as a super food. They are said to possess anti-inflammatory properties, and can help protect you against diabetes, cancer, and heart disease. Flaxseeds absorb water and expand into a gel after about twenty minutes. As such, this is a great option if you are looking for a thick smoothie, but don't like to take it thick, since it will expand in your stomach after drinking it.

The main quandary with flaxseed is that they have a tendency to spoil quickly. This means that you have to keep your flaxseeds in the refrigerator and use them relatively quickly before their lifespan expires. In addition, ground flaxseed is the best form of flaxseeds to take for maximum benefits.

Psyllium seed husks

You can also incorporate psyllium seed husks, which are packed with fiber, into your smoothie to thicken it. Like linseed and chia seeds, psyillium seed husks absorb liquid and swell up in your stomach to leave you feeling fuller for longer.

Xanthan gum

This is a natural carbohydrate that is often used to thicken food (for example in ice cream, sauces, and salad dressings), and in gluten free cooking. It is also very effective at reducing total cholesterol and blood sugar levels in diabetics (although it is advisable to check with your doctor before taking xanthan gum). It does not contain any flavor, and you will only need a little amount, about 1/8 to ¼ teaspoon. One tablespoon of xanthan gum contains 7 grams of fiber, 7 grams of carbohydrates, 30 calories, and no fat.

Frozen fruits

You can also add frozen fruits to thicken your smoothies a bit. Freezing fruit will not only add texture and thickness to your drink, but it will also enhance the flavors. Dense fruits are the most effective, including avocado, papaya, mangoes, and bananas. Water based ingredients such as watermelon will have the opposite effect.

Add nut butter/nuts

Add one tablespoon of nut butter (e.g. peanut butter) or a couple of nuts like walnuts, pecans, or almonds to your smoothie. You can soak the nuts in some water beforehand, in order to make them easier and softer to blend. Keep in mind that nuts can actually add calories to your smoothies. As such, add them only when you feel like your smoothie needs a few more healthy fats or calories, but do so sparingly.

Cut back on liquids

If you sense that a smoothie you are preparing is going to end up runny, reduce your liquid additions (for instance, juice, water, milk, and so on)

Other thickeners

- Coconut meat

- Beans (use black beans in dark or chocolate smoothies, and chickpeas or white beans in light colored smoothies such as vanilla or fruit).

- Irish moss

- LSA (prepared from almonds, sunflower seeds, and ground linseeds)

Smoothies are generally loaded with fiber, protein, and nutrients. As such, ensure that you also take a few glasses of water.

In order to lose weight, it is important to make balanced smoothies. This means making sure that there is protein, carbohydrate, water, dairy, fiber and basically all the necessary nutrients. Let us look closely at what you need to have in your smoothie to have a tasty and satiating smoothie that will help you lose weight.

Water/Milk

Of course, water has zero calories, and is probably the least calorie liquid you can incorporate into your smoothie, along with tea. However, while water does not contain any calories, it doesn't have any nutritional value. You can add some protein and micronutrients into your smoothie by adding coconut water (or some form of milk).

Below is a list of different liquids that you can add to your drink (each 1 cup), as well as their calorie content.

- Soymilk – 100 calories

- Skim milk – 80 calories

- Coconut water – 46 calories

- Almond milk – 35 calories

- Hemp-milk – 100 calories

- Rice milk – 120 calories

- 1 percent milk – 110 calories

- Vanilla rice milk – 130 calories

- 2 percent milk – 130 calories

- Oat milk – 130 calories

- Whole milk – 150 calories

Carbohydrates (and fiber)

Fruits and veggies will form most of your fiber and carbohydrate intake, as well as nutrients in your smoothies. While fruit make smoothies tastier, they tend to have more calories than vegetables. Ensure that you monitor your portion sizes when it comes to adding fruit. Limit yourself to two cups per serving of fruit, and if you can, incorporate leafy vegetables into your smoothie.

Protein

Ensure that you include protein in your smoothie, if you are planning to replace it with a certain meal (for instance, breakfast). Protein will keep you feeling full and make your drink seem more like a real meal. Protein also helps to maintain your muscle mass, some of which is lost together with body fat as you try to lose weight. The amount of protein you are consuming will dictate how much muscle you'll lose. What's more, if you are exercising, adding protein to your smoothies will help your muscles recover from your exercise and maximize the results. Excellent low calorie sources of protein include:

- Beans

- Protein powder (brown rice protein, hemp, or whey)

- Ricotta cheese

- Cottage cheese

- Silken tofu

- Kefir

- Yogurt

Fat

Fat is probably one of the most misunderstood nutrients in the world. While it is true that fat is rich in calories, taking moderate amounts can be great for your health, and even help you lose weight. Healthy fat enhances the absorption of certain vitamins into your body, and is essential for general good health, proper growth, and development. In addition, fat adds flavor to smoothies, and, most importantly, helps you feel less hungry and more satisfied. In fact, some healthy fats, such as avocado and olive oil, can actually contribute to weight loss around the belly. In order to ensure that you are enjoying the benefits of fats, make sure you're using healthy fats (polyunsaturated/monounsaturated). Add one tablespoon of fat, if your smoothie does not contain any fat:

- Tahini (sesame paste)

- Chia seeds

- Flaxseed oil/flax seeds

- Coconut oil

- Avocado

Sweeten, if you have to

Purchased smoothies tend to contain a lot of added sugar, and some can even have several times the recommended daily amount in a single smoothie.

As a general rule of thumb, try to stick to ripe fruits for your smoothies, which will provide enough sugar for your drink, without having to sweeten it any further. You can also add spices such as nutmeg and cinnamon, or extracts such as almond and vanilla that will sweeten your drink without adding more calories. If it is absolutely necessary to add some extra sweetness to your drink, use natural sweeteners such as xylitol (sugar like taste with additional health benefits) and stevia (zero calories). You can also try using maple syrup, molasses, or honey, which are lower in calories, but packed with important nutrients. Here is a list of different sweeteners (two tablespoons each) and their calorie content:

- Blackstrap molasses – 32 calories

- Xylitol – 20 calories

- Stevia – 0 calories

- Maple syrup – 45 calories

- Honey – 43 calories

To enhance flavor without adding more calories

The following fresh herbs, extracts, and spices can help you boost the nutritional power and flavor of your smoothie without increasing the calorie content:

- Basil

- Lavender

- Parsley (green smoothies)

- Ginger

- Cardamom

- Cinnamon

- Allspice

- Almond extract

- Peppermint/Mint extract

- Lemongrass

- Coriander/Cilantro

- Lemon/lime juice

- Clove

- Cayenne pepper

- Nutmeg

- Vanilla extract

- Coconut extract

Weight loss boosters

Green tea

This works as a superb low calorie base for any smoothie, in addition to the fact that it helps boost metabolism. Green tea has been shown to contain antioxidants known as catechins that enhance fat burning, and increase weight loss. The additional bonus is that green tea can also reduce your LDL cholesterol (bad fat) levels.

Cinnamon

This is a tasty way for boosting the sweetness and flavor of your drink without the risk of increasing the calorie content. In addition, cinnamon has been shown to reduce the rate at which your stomach digests meals, which subsequently helps keep your blood glucose levels more stable, and leaves you feeling satisfied for longer.

Dark chocolate

Dark chocolate has been shown to reduce the concentration of a stress hormone known as cortisol, which tends to promote fat storage, particularly in the belly region. Use unsweetened cocoa nibs or cocoa powder.

Ginger

Ginger is packed with active ingredients that have a similar structure as capsaicin, a compound in hot peppers that has been shown to boost metabolism. Ginger has also been shown to improve digestion, apart from boosting metabolism. Add one tablespoon of fresh ground ginger into your drink for a little kick.

Vinegar

Vinegar reduces the rate at which food passes from the stomach to the small intestine, thus making you feel fuller for a longer period. In addition, taking one or two tablespoons of vinegar on a regular basis has been associated with a smaller waist and reduced body weight. Incorporating vinegar into your smoothie will also provide a little acidic flavor – something reminiscent to a lemon squeeze.

Chili pepper

These contain a compound known as capsaicin, which has been shown to increase energy levels, boost metabolism, and curb appetite.

Yogurt

Yogurt can boost your weight loss efforts as well, especially in the belly region. Studies have shown that, apart from increasing fat loss, yogurt can also help delay the loss of muscles that is usually associated with weight loss.

Weight Loss Smoothies

Pound pounds away smoothie (73.6 calories per serving)

Servings: 1

Ingredients

1 large tomato

½ carrot

¼ small onion

2 sprigs cilantro

1 cup spinach

½ stalk celery

½ bell pepper

¼ lime

1 ½ cups water

Directions

Combine all the ingredients in your NutriBullet, and process until smooth. Serve and enjoy!

Slimming citrus blast (163 calories per serving)

Servings: 1

Ingredients

¼ grapefruit

3 strawberries

1 tablespoon chia seeds

2 handfuls spinach

1 orange

¼ cup raspberries

1 ½ cups water

Directions

Combine all the ingredients in a NutriBullet, and puree until smooth. Enjoy!

Incorporating more vegetables and fruits in your diet is the best way to shed off unnecessary weight. Low glycemic fruits such as the grapefruit and strawberries in this recipe go a long way towards weight loss.

Fat burning green tea smoothie (68 calories per serving)

Servings: 1

Ingredients

2 cauliflower florets

3 broccoli florets

2 pineapple spears

Green tea to the fill line

Directions

Combine all the ingredients in the NutriBullet, and blend until smooth, about 20 to 30 seconds.

Serve and enjoy.

Blueberry peach smoothie (68 calories per serving)

Servings: 2

Ingredients

1½ cups of frozen peaches or fresh sliced peach, pits removed

½ cup fresh or frozen blueberries

About ¾ cup of unsweetened vanilla almond milk

Directions

Combine everything in the NutriBullet, and blend until smooth.

Strawberry peach green smoothie (255 calories per serving)

Servings: 1

Ingredients

½ cup frozen strawberries

1 small handful of spinach

Peach mango juice to the fill line

½ cup frozen peaches

Directions

Combine everything into your NutriBullet and process until you achieve a smooth consistency.

Rainbow berry blast (79 calories per serving)

Servings: 2

Ingredients

½ medium pomegranate

1 cup rainbow chard

½ cup berry mix (blackberries, raspberries, blueberries)

½ cup of unsweetened coconut milk to the max line

Directions

Combine all the ingredients in the NutriBullet, and process until smooth.

Tropical protein shake (190 calories per serving)

Servings: 2

Ingredients

1 medium kiwi, skin intact

1 cup vanilla Greek yogurt

6 almonds

1 cup fresh pineapple

2 tablespoons of unsweetened coconut

Coconut milk to the fill line

Directions

Combine all the ingredients in the NutriBullet, and process until smooth.

Strawberry chocolate blast (181 calories per serving)

Servings: 1

Ingredients

6 strawberries

¼ beet

1 ½ cups of unsweetened almond milk

1 handful spinach

2 teaspoons of raw cacao powder

1 tablespoon super food protein blend

Directions

Toss everything in the NutriBullet and process until smooth. Serve in a glass and enjoy!

Strawberry and oat smoothie (153 calories per serving)

Servings: 1

Ingredients

½ medium pear, cored and sliced

½ cup low-fat milk

½ cup strawberries, halved

2 tablespoons of rolled oats

Directions

Combine the low fat milk, rolled oats, pear, and strawberries in your NutriBullet and blend until smooth, about ten to twelve seconds. Serve in a chilled glass, and garnish with a slice of pear or strawberry, if desired.

Low fat banana smoothie (175 calories per serving)

Servings: 1

Ingredients

1 small banana, sliced

½ cup skim milk

¼ teaspoon of cinnamon, ground

2 tablespoons of rolled oats

Directions

Combine the skim milk, rolled oats, banana, and cinnamon in your NutriBullet and blend until smooth, about ten to twelve seconds. Serve in a chilled glass, and garnish with a banana slice, if desired.

Coconut banana and strawberry smoothie (121 calories per serving)

Servings: 1

Ingredients

1 cup strawberries, frozen

½ medium banana, sliced

Coconut water to max line

Directions

Combine the coconut water, strawberries, and banana in the NutriBullet and blend until smooth, about ten to twelve seconds. Serve in a chilled glass, and add strawberry to garnish, if desired.

Grapefruit and lime smoothie (90 calories per serving)

Servings: 1

Ingredients

½ medium grapefruit, cut into segments

½ cup watermelon, cubed

1 tablespoon of lime juice

1-2 ice cubes

Coconut water to max line

Directions

Combine the coconut water, lime juice, grapefruit, and watermelon in the NutriBullet and blend until smooth, about ten to twelve seconds. Serve in a chilled glass, and garnish with a grapefruit or slice of watermelon, if desired.

Blueberry tofu smoothie (364 calories per serving)

Servings: 1

Ingredients

½ banana

½ cup nonfat plain yogurt

1 cup soft Tofu

½ cup nonfat milk

½ cup blueberries, frozen

Directions

Combine the banana, blueberries, yogurt, milk, and tofu in a NutriBullet, and process until lightly smooth.

Banana strawberry smoothie (119 calories per serving)

Servings: 2

Ingredients

½ fresh banana, sliced

8 oz. flavored water, any flavor

1 cup Strawberries, frozen

6-8 oz. yogurt

1 cup ice

Directions

Combine the flavored water, yogurt, banana, frozen strawberries, and ice in a NutriBullet, and process until smooth. Serve in a glass immediately, adding water if necessary.

Watermelon and tomato cooler with hemp seed (77 calories per serving)

Servings: 1

Ingredients

1 medium tomato, sliced

1 teaspoon hemp seeds

¾ cup watermelon, diced

¼ medium carrot, diced

Water to max line

Crushed ice, to serve

Directions

Combine the hemp seeds, carrot, tomato, and watermelon in the Nutribullet then add water to the max line. Puree in the NutriBullet until smooth, about ten to twelve seconds. Serve in a glass with ice, and garnish with watermelon, if desired.

Pineapple and banana with mint smoothie (154 calories per serving)

Servings: 1

Ingredients

1 small banana, sliced

1 mint sprig

½ cup pineapple, diced

½ cup coconut water

¼ cup crushed ice

Directions

Combine the crushed ice, mint, coconut water, banana, and pineapple in the NutriBullet until smooth, about ten to twelve seconds. Pour into a serving glass and serve garnished with banana or slice of pineapple, if desired.

Spiced banana pineapple and soy yogurt shake (198 calories per serving)

Servings: 1

Ingredients

½ cup pineapple, diced

½ cup soy yogurt, plain or vanilla

5g fresh ginger, sliced

½ banana, sliced

Water to max line

Directions

Combine the soy yogurt, banana, pineapple, and ginger in the Nutribullet and blend until smooth, about ten to twelve minutes.

Serve in a glass, and garnish with a slice of pineapple or ginger. Enjoy!

Spiced banana and melon with hemp seed (124 calories per serving)

Servings: 1

Ingredients

¾ cup melon, diced

1 teaspoon hemp seeds

Crushed ice, to serve

5g fresh ginger, sliced

½ sliced medium banana

Water to max line

Directions

Combine the hemp seeds, banana, melon, and hemp seeds in the Nutribullet, and add water to the max line. Blend until smooth, about ten to twelve seconds.

Pineapple and kiwi with almond smoothie (155 calories per serving)

Servings: 1

Ingredients

1 medium kiwi fruit, sliced

½ cup almond milk

½ medium banana, sliced

½ cup pineapple, diced

Directions

Mix the almond milk, pineapple, kiwi fruit, and banana in the Nutribullet and blend until smooth, about ten to twelve seconds. Serve in a chilled glass, and garnish with kiwi fruit or a slice of banana, if desired.

Avocado and pineapple smoothie (190 calories per serving)

Servings: 1

Ingredients

½ medium banana, sliced

½ cup skim milk

1/8 medium avocado, sliced

½ cup pineapple, diced

Directions

Put the skim milk, pineapple, banana, and avocado in the Nutribullet and blend for ten to twelve seconds, or until smooth. Serve in a chilled glass, and garnish with a banana or slice of avocado, if desired. Enjoy!

Creamy banana flax raspberry smoothie (163 calories per serving)

Servings: 1

Ingredients

½ medium banana, sliced

¼ cup Greek yogurt

½ cup raspberries

1 teaspoon of flaxseeds

¼ cup skim milk

Directions

Mix the skim milk, Greek yogurt, flaxseeds, banana, and raspberries in a Nutribullet and blend for ten to twelve seconds, or until smooth. Serve in a glass, and garnish with a few raspberries, if desired.

Blueberry and almond shake with flaxseed (91 calories per serving)

Servings: 1

Ingredients

1 medium tomato, sliced

1 teaspoon of flaxseeds

½ cup blueberries, frozen

½ cup almond milk

Directions

Put the flaxseeds, almond milk, tomato, and blueberries in the Nutribullet and blend until smooth, about ten to twelve seconds. Serve in a glass, and garnish with a few blueberries, if desired.

The flaxseeds, almond milk, tomato, and blueberries in this recipe are great for digestion because of their high fiber concentration, which promotes normal bowel movement.

Kiwi lemon lettuce smoothie (54 calories per serving)

Servings: 1

Ingredients

2 tablespoons of lemon juice

¾ cup green tea, freshly brewed

1 medium kiwi fruit, sliced

2 lettuce leaves

Directions

Combine the green tea, lettuce, lemon juice, and kiwi fruit in the Nutribullet and blend until smooth, about ten seconds. Serve in a chilled glass, and garnish with a piece of lemon or kiwi fruit, if desired.

Apple banana and avocado with mint (196 calories per serving)

Servings: 1

Ingredients

1/8 medium avocado, sliced

1 mint sprig

½ medium apple, cored and sliced

½ medium banana, sliced

½ cup skim milk

Directions

Mix the mint, banana, avocado, and apple in the Nutribullet, and process until smooth, about ten seconds. Serve in a chilled glass, and garnish with mint sprig (optional).

This recipe is loaded with fiber, which is beneficial for your digestive system.

Mixed almond berry and fennel with sunflower seeds (85 calories per serving)

Servings: 1

Ingredients

½ cup fennel bulb, shredded

1 tablespoon of sunflower seeds

½ cup mixed berries

½ cup almond milk

Directions

Combine the sunflower seeds, almond milk, fennel bulb, and mixed berries in the NutriBullet and blend until smooth, about ten seconds. Serve in a chilled glass, and garnish with mixed berries (optional).

Blueberry high protein smoothie (425 calories per serving)

Servings: 1

Ingredients

2/3 cup blueberries

6 oz. silken tofu soft

1 tablespoon of honey

1 medium banana

Soy milk to fill line

Directions

Combine all the ingredients in the NutriBullet, except for the soymilk. Add the soymilk last, and fill it to the max line. Process until smooth.

This recipe is packed with protein, and is an excellent post workout meal or food replacement. Taking protein after exercise help to boost your muscles after the workout. Mixing some carbohydrates with your protein will also help slow down the breakdown. The ingredients in this recipe will also help your body replenish the used minerals and vitamins, as well as obtain the following: 21 percent Iron, 52 percent calcium, 45 percent Vitamin D, Vitamin B complex, and many others.

Healthy Breakfast Smoothie

Servings: 1

Ingredients

¼ green apple

Juice of ½ lemon

1 small piece of pineapple

¼ cup of water

1 orange

¼ red apple

1 small piece of fresh ginger, to taste

1 teaspoon of honey

Put all the ingredients into the NutriBullet, and process until smooth, about thirty seconds.

The warming flavors of ginger and honey will sooth your throat, while the pineapple, carrot, and orange will provide you with vitamin C

Raspberry sorbet

Servings: 1

Ingredients

3 tablespoons water

1 cup raspberries

2 teaspoons honey

Directions

Put all the ingredients into the NutriBullet, and pulse until desired consistency. Enjoy!

Lean green smoothie

Servings: 1

Ingredients

3 sprigs parsley

½ stalk celery

½ inch ginger

1 ½ cups water

½ cup kale

2 chunks cucumber

½ pear

1 splash apple cider vinegar

Directions

Combine all the ingredients in the NutriBullet, and extract until smooth, about thirty seconds. Enjoy!

Thirst quencher

Servings: 1

Ingredients

½ cup mangos

10 almonds

1 cup spinach

½ medium banana

½ inch ginger

Green tea to max line

Directions

Combine all the ingredients in your NutriBullet, and process until smooth, about thirty seconds.

Enjoy!

This smoothie will increase your antioxidant and nutrient intake, while helping you hydrate at the same time. Apart from helping you hydrate, green tea is also packed with antioxidants that will help your body fight certain types of cancers, maintain your energy, and boost your heart health.

Mango sorbet

Servings: 1

½ inch ginger

¾ cup coconut water

1 cup mango, frozen

1 tablespoon maple syrup

Directions

Combine all the ingredients into your NutriBullet, and process until smooth. Enjoy!

Blueberry Greek yogurt smoothie

Servings: 1

Ingredients

2 teaspoons honey

½ lemon, juiced

2 cups blueberries

½ cup Greek yogurt

3 ice cubes

Directions

Put all the ingredients into your NutriBullet, and process until smooth. Enjoy!

Mint peach blast

Servings: 1

Ingredients

1 peach

½ teaspoon honey

1 handful kale

3 leaves mint

1 teaspoon Superfood chia seeds

Green tea to max line

Directions

Prepare the green tea first, and then blend with the other ingredients in your NutriBullet until smooth. Enjoy!

Mint adds flavor to this smoothie, and provides you with a wide range of health benefits, such as digestion calming, immune boosting, and anti-inflammatory properties. Peaches have many health benefits, such as supporting overall heart health, reducing wrinkles, combating free radicals, and providing plenty of vitamin C.

Watermelon milkshake

Servings: 1

Ingredients

½ banana

½ tablespoon honey

1 cup coconut milk

1 ½ cups watermelon

½ lemon (juiced)

½ teaspoon vanilla extract

Directions

Combine all the ingredients in the NutriBullet, and process until smooth. Enjoy!

Coconut milk provides smoothness and creaminess to this drink, in addition to providing plenty of magnesium, calcium, vitamins, and more.

Nutribullet Smoothie Recipes For Radiant Skin

The skin care industry makes billions of dollars every year from susceptible repeat customers looking to making their skin softer and healthier. However, what you may not realize is that the foods you eat can affect your skin just as much, or even more than the creams and cleansers you apply topically. Let us look at foods that are great for you skin and that you can include in your smoothies.

Carrots

Carrots are high in vitamin A – beta carotene, which is a very potent antioxidant that helps to maintain a youthful appearance, slow aging, and stop cells from degenerating. In addition, vitamin A helps your body maintain tissue growth, as well as healthy vision, teeth, and bones. Carrots are also relatively rich in vitamin C, which supports the production of collagen in your body. Collagen is vital for slowing the signs of aging, preventing wrinkles, and for skin elasticity.

Carrots are also packed with potassium, which contributes to the production of new skin cells, subsequently helping your body prevent and heal dark spots or scars on your skin, reduce blemishes/acne, and maintain the right electrolyte balance. Lastly, carrots contain antioxidants that help flush out toxins from your liver, preventing them from manifesting on your face as acne!

Parsley

This popular herb is loaded with vitamin A and C. It helps maintain a level skin tone by clearing blemishes and acne, while also cleansing your kidneys, liver, and urinary tract. Parsley also contains high amounts of vitamin K, which has been proven to accelerate the process of wound healing, as well as improving skin elasticity.

Tofu

As you age, your skin loses its ability to "bounce back", due to low levels of collagen. Tofu, which is packed with protein, vitamin E, and calcium, has the ability to maintain skin elasticity by reducing the rate at which your body loses collagen.

Berries

These include Goji berries, blueberries, raspberries, and strawberries. Generally, the darker it is, the more beneficial it is. Darker berries contain higher levels of antioxidants (which fight free radicals caused by such things as pollution and UV damage), as well as healthy vitamin C that can boost your collagen supply.

Tomatoes

You are probably aware that tomatoes are great for your blood and heart health, but studies have confirmed that these are also helpful in protecting against aging skin and sun damage. Tomatoes contain a phytochemical known as lycopene (which is responsible for their red appearance), that boosts the protection of your skin from the sun, and minimizes damage from exposure. It is also believed to stimulate the production and circulation of collagen for a youthful face.

Seeds

There is a wide variety of seeds to choose from like hemp seeds, chia seeds, pumpkin seeds, sunflower seeds, and flaxseeds. All these seeds contain skin-boosting properties. They are loaded with selenium and vitamin E, and can help you achieve a gorgeous complexion. These seeds are also bursting with really potent antioxidants, protein, and omega 3 and 6.

Spinach, broccoli, and Brussels sprouts

These green leafy vegetables are packed with alpha lipoic acid (ALA), a very powerful anti-aging agent that is concentrated with potent antioxidants. It also contains anti-inflammatory properties, reducing under eye circles, blotches, redness, and puffiness, while limiting the appearance of wrinkles at the same time.

Grapefruit

These are high in vitamin C, which helps reverse the damage done by pollutants and the sun on your skin. It also stimulates the production of collagen, leading to a generally smoother texture, reduced wrinkles, and new skin growth.

Banana

Bananas are packed with moisture, vitamins E & C, and potassium that can help hydrate and moisturize your skin, leaving it soft and supple. Bananas also contain certain nutrients that help fight wrinkles on your face and prevent the appearance of fine lines. In addition, bananas have been shown to treat pimples and acne, and lighten dark spots that tend to make your face look dull.

Honey

Honey contains natural antibacterial properties, and is great for the prevention and treatment of acne. It is also packed with antioxidants, which help slow down the aging process. In addition, it is extremely soothing and moisturizing, which helps keep your skin glowing. Honey also tends to open up pores and make it easier to unclog them.

Papayas

Papayas are an excellent source of Papain and vitamin A, which helps get rid of dead skin cells and break down inactive proteins. In addition, they have a low sodium quality, which helps to hydrate your skin. Papayas have a higher concentration of carotene than apples, plantains, guava, and custard apples, which makes it a beneficial wholesome fruit. Let us look at tasty smoothies that you can make using your nutribullet for healthier and beautiful skin.

Kale me beautiful (233 calories per serving)

Servings: 1

Ingredients

¼ red bell pepper

½ cup strawberries

1 tablespoon chia seeds

1 cup almond milk

1 cup kale

½ cup raspberries

½ cup silken tofu

1 tablespoon almonds

Coconut water to max line

Directions

Combine all the ingredients in the NutriBullet and blend until smooth, about forty seconds. The combination of red bell pepper and kale provides a wealth of antioxidant carotenoids, while the tofu is rich in magnesium and selenium, which are great for skin health.

Anti-aging coconut blast

Servings: 1

Ingredients

1 banana, frozen

½ teaspoon turmeric

½ teaspoon ginger

1 teaspoon maca powder

½ cup pineapple, frozen

1 tablespoon coconut oil

½ teaspoon cinnamon

1 teaspoon chia seeds

1 cup coconut milk

Directions

Combine all the ingredients in your NutriBullet, and process until smooth. Serve in a glass and enjoy!

Turmeric is a proven inflammation fighter, which helps reduce skin redness and various other irritants. Coconuts, on the other hand, contain anti-inflammatory and antioxidant properties that help fight the signs of aging, while chia seeds are packed with omega 3 oils that are very effective against numerous skin conditions.

Pretty NutriBlast (439 calories per serving)

Servings: 1

Ingredients

¼ cup almonds

1 cup almond milk

¼ cup goji berries

2 tablespoons cacao

Directions

Put all the ingredients in the Nutribullet, and process until smooth.

Goji berries are very rich in nutrients, and are one of the most powerful antioxidants. Raw cacao, on the other hand, is a great source of beautifying iron, calcium, and magnesium.

Lemon lavender blast (264 calories per serving)

Servings: 1

Ingredients

1 cup blueberries

1 tablespoon lemon juice

1 teaspoon chia seeds

1 banana, frozen

1 teaspoon lavender flowers

½ teaspoon lemon zest

1 ½ cups almond milk

Directions

Combine all the ingredients in your Nutribullet and process until smooth, about forty seconds. Enjoy!

Lavender has been shown to help with digestive problems and is believed to contain anti-inflammatory and antiseptic properties.

Chocolate chia seed pudding (544 calories per serving)

Servings: 1

Ingredients

2 tablespoons cacao powder

½ teaspoon vanilla extract

2 tablespoons chia seeds

2 tablespoons raw, organic honey

¾ cup almond milk

Directions

Combine all the ingredients in your NutriBullet, and process until smooth. Place in the refrigerator for about one to two hours to chill. Add your favorite toppings – e.g. almond pieces, coconut flakes, cacao nibs, and so forth.

Chia seeds are high in nutrients, low in calories, and loaded with fiber. They are great for satiating and thus a wonderful breakfast addition. They are also high in protein and packed with antioxidants.

Avocado blueberry blast (248 calories per serving)

Servings: 1

Ingredients

1 cup blueberries

½ lime

1 handful spinach

¼ avocado

Coconut water to max line

Directions

Combine all the ingredients in your Nutribullet and process until smooth.

The monounsaturated fatty acids in avocado can lower your cholesterol levels and reduce your risk of heart disease, while the phytochemicals and antioxidants in blueberries will help you fight back disease.

Papaya pineapple blast (493 calories per serving)

Servings: 1

Ingredients

½ cup papayas

3 strawberries

1 handful cashews

1 cup mixed greens

½ cup pineapple

½ teaspoon coconut oil

1 ½ cups coconut water

Directions

Combine all the ingredients in your Nutribullet and blend for 15 seconds or until smooth.

This recipe is rich in antioxidants and vitamin C, and can help your body beat infection and prevent chronic heart illness.

Nutribullet Energy Boosting Smoothie Recipes

Feeling fatigued most of the time. You are not alone. Family obligations, long working hours, an inability to get adequate sleep, and hectic schedules can easily leave you frazzled like a clapped up camel. However, before you reach for that highly caffeinated energy drink for a quick boost, it is important to consider other lifestyle factors, including your diet. Your energy levels are influenced by what you eat and how you live your life on a daily basis. Incorporating your morning smoothie with the right foods can really go a long way towards boosting your energy levels for the rest of the day, as well as adding to your general wellbeing, health, and nutrition. Before we look at some smoothies to take for an energy boost, let us first understand what causes fatigue.

What causes fatigue?

In most cases, low energy levels can be attributed to lifestyle factors such as diet, stress, high activity, and lack of sleep. These are easy to reverse, but chronic fatigue could be a sign of an underlying health complication. Consider paying your doctor a visit if you seem to be tired all the time, no matter how much rest you get. It could be a sign of a mood (mental) disorder (such as depression), or physical illness such as anemia, kidney disease, hypothyroidism, chronic fatigue syndrome, to name just a few.

Fatigue can also occur when your adrenal glands experience a general state of dysfunction. These glands are located above your kidneys, and their work is to release hormones during stress. They play a role in the fight or flight response, where your body reacts to a threatening situation by choosing to either fight or run away. Chronic stress can lead to a situation known as adrenal fatigue, where your adrenal glands fail to meet the required hormone production because of being overworked. This, in turn, can leave you feeling fatigued and worn out.

Energy Boosting Ingredients For Your Smoothies

Nuts & nut butters

Generally, nuts are packed with energy (in the form of calories) from healthy fats and protein. In addition, nuts are rich in micronutrients (e.g. magnesium and selenium in Brazil nuts) that your body needs to make the most of energy sources.

Coconut oil

Extra virgin coconut oil has an array of health benefits, one of which is the ability to boost your energy levels. Coconut oil consists of fatty acids, like all oils. However, unlike most of the oils you use, it is mostly made up of medium chain fatty acids, which are smaller molecules that can be absorbed easily by your body and used for instant energy.

Leafy greens

The darkest greens are generally the most nutritious. However, any leafy green can provide you with a burst of the vitamins B complex, A, C, and K. Greens are also packed with fiber, folic acid, and iron, all of which work together to provide lasting energy.

Citrus fruits

Grapefruits, oranges, lemons, and limes are loaded with vitamin C, which has been shown to enhance the immune system. You need a healthy, working immune system for sufficient energy. It is common to feel run down when it is not working properly.

Greek yogurt

Greek yogurt contains a significantly higher amount of protein than most other forms of yogurt, and this can help maintain your energy levels throughout the day. Without protein, it can be easy to feel really drained. Apart from this, yogurt is packed with probiotics, which are great for your immune system.

Let us now look at some tasty smoothies;

Beet and pineapple with parsley Smoothie (99 calories per serving)

Servings: 1

Ingredients

½ cup pineapple, diced

¼ cup parsley

1 medium beet root, sliced

5g ginger, sliced

Water to max line

Directions

Mix the parsley, ginger, pineapple, and beetroot in the nutribullet then add water to the max line. Blend until smooth, about ten seconds. Serve in a glass, and garnish with a piece of ginger or beet root, if desired. Enjoy!

Easy nectarine mixed coconut and berry shake (125 calories per serving)

Servings: 1

Ingredients

½ cup mixed berries, frozen

1 medium nectarine, sliced

½ cup coconut water

Crushed ice, to serve

Directions

Combine the coconut water, mixed berries, and nectarine in your Nutribullet and blend until smooth, about ten seconds. Serve in a glass with crushed ice, and garnish with some mixed berries or a slice of nectarine, if desired.

Cherry and cereal with hemp seeds (105 calories per serving)

Servings: 1

Ingredients

½ cup almond milk

1 teaspoon of hemp seeds

½ cup fresh cherries, pitted

2 tablespoons of rolled oats

Directions

Mix the hemp seeds, rolled oats, almond milk, and cherries in the NutriBullet and blend until smooth, about ten to twelve seconds.

Serve in a glass, and garnish with cherry (optional).

The ingredients in this recipe are diabetic friendly and tasty, and will keep you invigorated for the better part of the day.

Energy boosting blast (233 calories per serving)

Servings: 1

Ingredients

1 banana

1 clementine

1 handful spinach

1 cup mixed berries

1 tablespoon super-food energy boost

Coconut water to max line

Directions

Put all the ingredients in the Nutribullet and process until smooth.

Hazelnut coffee smoothie (374 calories per serving)

Servings: 1

Ingredients

1 medium frozen banana

¼ cup chopped hazelnuts

1 stevia packet

8 fl oz of iced coffee

½ cup plain nonfat Greek yogurt

1 teaspoon of vanilla

Directions

Put all the ingredients in the NutriBullet cup, and add the iced coffee up to the fill line. Process until smooth and consistent. Serve garnished with chocolate and whipped cream

The combination of hazelnuts and coffee provides a tasty smoothie that can be taken as a dessert or a snack. The hazelnuts are packed with dietary fiber for a healthy digestive system, as well as healthy fats that have been proven to prevent strokes and heart disease. The Greek yogurt, on the other hand, provides a creamy texture that's loaded with protein..

Energizing NutriBullet smoothie (466 calories per serving)

Servings: 1

Ingredients

1 tablespoon of pumpkin seeds

½ avocado, pitted and peeled

½ cup Greek yogurt

1 tablespoon of raw organic almond butter

1 cup organic kale

½ cup grapefruit juice

Water to fill line

Directions

Combine all the ingredients in the NutriBullet, with the water going last. Fill the water to the max fill line, and process the ingredients until they reach the desired consistency.

The yogurt in this smoothie is rich in the vitamin B complex, which is great for keeping your body energized. The other ingredients provide high quality proteins that can help increase your resilience during strenuous activities. This smoothie is also packed with omega 6 fatty acids, totaling up to 5.47grams.

Lemon avocado green smoothie

Servings: 1

Ingredients

1 large banana, sliced

1 lime wedge

2 tablespoons avocado

1 tablespoon of honey

1 cup spinach

2 lemon wedges

2 tablespoons of cashews

2 tablespoons of coconut butter

Milk to fill line

Directions

Put all the ingredients in your NutriBullet, and process until smooth.

Although lemons are commonly used as a garnish and flavoring for food, they are packed with vitamins (eg. Vitamin C) and antioxidants, and help prevent the development of cancer by hindering the multiplication of cancer cells. Lime also provides additional vitamin C, while spinach and avocado make this recipe green and smooth.

Carrot, banana smoothie (378 calories per serving)

Servings: 1

Ingredients

1 tablespoon of ground flax seeds

1 orange, peeled

1 banana, halved

¼ teaspoon of pumpkin seeds

2 cups spinach

1 carrot, thoroughly washed

½ cup Greek Yogurt

Low fat milk to the fill line

Directions

Combine all the ingredients in the NutriBullet, with the low fat milk going last. Blend the ingredients until desired consistency.

The ingredients in this recipe provide essential nutrients that have been associated with enhanced metabolism. These include coenzyme Q10, iron, L-carnitine, and B-complex. One serving provides 10 percent vitamin B3, 34 percent DV vitamin B2, 21 percent DV vitamin B1, and 150 percent DV vitamin A. Flax seeds and pumpkins seeds in this recipe provide omega 3 and proteins.

Strawberry kiwi smoothie

Servings: 1

Ingredients

1 cup of strawberries

1 teaspoon of orange juice

2 kiwis

1 tablespoon of honey

1 teaspoon of vanilla extract

Almond milk to fill line

Directions

Combine all the ingredients in your Nutribullet, and process until smooth.

Kiwi is a very alkaline fruit, which means that it is very rich in minerals. As such, kiwis have the ability to diminish and replace the acidity in your body, and subsequently help you prevent osteoporosis and arthritis, reduce insomnia, and maintain a youthful and healthy skin. In addition, honey provides you with a great kick of energy.

Gingered apple carrot smoothie (112 calories per serving)

Servings: 1

Ingredients

1 medium carrot, sliced

1 tablespoon lemon juice

¼ teaspoon of allspice

5 g ginger

1 medium apple, cored and sliced

½ teaspoon of cinnamon

¼ teaspoon of nutmeg

Water to fill line

Directions

Combine all the ingredients in the NutriBullet cup, with water going last to fill up to the fill line. Blend the ingredients until you achieve the desired consistency.

The ginger in this recipe has been used for herbal purposes since time immemorial, and has been shown to reduce inflammation, and cure nausea, motion sickness, and upset stomach. This smoothie will provide you with 28 percent manganese, 15 percent vitamin C and 30 percent vitamin A (DV).

Nutty peanut butter hazelnut smoothie (550 calories per serving)

Servings: 1

Ingredients

2 tablespoons of peanut butter

5 ice cubes

1/3 cup toasted hazelnuts

1 tablespoon of honey

Milk to fill line

Directions

Combine all the ingredients in your NutriBullet, and process until smooth.

Hazelnuts are packed with unsaturated fats, which are great for the heart. As such, hazelnuts help your body maintain proper amounts of calcium and cholesterol in your body.

Nutribullet Smoothie Recipes For A Healthy Heart And Immune System

The best way to avoid infections and fight disease-causing organisms is to maintain a healthy immune system. The natural defense systems in your body are designed to recognize, fight, and get rid of foreign invaders such as viruses and bacteria.

However, regardless of this, your immune system is not perfect. Eating certain foods can help it remain in top form and enhance its effectiveness.

Countless microbes live in your body, but most of them are not dangerous, and are even beneficial. However, several other bacteria, viruses, fungi, and parasites can make you sick.

Your immune system needs most of the nutrients in the ingredients you'll be using for your smoothies, in order to function properly. Some of the most important nutrients for this purpose include the minerals zinc and selenium, and vitamins A, B2, B6, C, D & E. Great immune boosters you should use in your smoothies include:

Blueberries

Blueberries are high in antioxidants. Antioxidants play a major role in maintaining a functional immune system. They combat the effects of free radicals in your body to help keep you healthy. They include zinc, selenium, polyphenols, and vitamins C & E. Other berries that contain antioxidants are blackberries, cranberries, strawberries, and raspberries.

Acai berries

These contain a higher concentration of antioxidants than even blueberries, but are relatively hard to find. They are mainly found in the Amazon, and are probably the most antioxidant-rich foods in the world.

Goji berries

Goji berries have been shown to contain certain compounds known as polysaccharides, which can actually boost your immune system.

Pumpkin

This is a brilliant addition to your smoothie, which is packed with vitamin A. Vitamin A has several functions in your body, one of which is facilitating communication between cells in order for your immune system to recognize and distinguish normal, healthy cells from the invaders. Vitamin A is also helpful in maintaining a fit respiratory tract.

Hemp seeds

The nutritional benefits of hemp seeds were ignored for a long time because of their botanical association with medicinal/drug varieties of cannabis. However, hempseeds don't have any psychotropic side effects. In fact, their unique nutritional profile can actually provide you with significant health benefits including:

- Naturally reducing sugar cravings and cleansing your colon.

- It is a "perfect protein", containing all twenty amino acids, as well as the nine essential amino acids that your body needs but cannot produce.

- Being rich in gamma linolenic acid (or GLA) – a significant omega 6 fatty acid derived from egg yolks and borage oil that has been shown to help balance hormones naturally.

- Excellent balance of omega 3 to omega 6 fatty acids, with a ratio of 3:1, which helps promote cardiovascular health.

- They are packed with phytonutrients that include:

Minerals

Iron (14 milligrams per 100 grams)

Manganese (7 milligrams per 100 grams)

Potassium (859 milligrams per 100 grams)

Calcium (145 milligrams per 100 grams)

Magnesium (483 milligrams per 100 grams)

Phosphorus (1160 milligrams per 100 grams)

Zinc (7 milligrams per 100 grams)

Vitamins

Vitamin B1 (0.4 milligrams per 100 grams)

Vitamin B3 (2.8 milligrams per 100 grams)

Vitamin D (22.77.5 IU milligrams/100 grams)

Vitamin A (3800 IU milligrams/100 grams)

Vitamin B2 (0.11 milligrams/100 grams)

Vitamin B6 (0.12 milligrams/100 grams)

Vitamin E (90 IU milligrams/100 grams)

Let us now look at tasty smoothies that can improve your immunity and heart health.

Blueberry avocado blast

Servings: 1

Ingredients

¼ avocado

1 tablespoon of super food cleansing greens

1 cup coconut water

½ cup of Greek yogurt

1 cup blueberries

2 tablespoons lime juice

1 tablespoon honey

1 Handful Ice Cubes

Directions

Combine all the ingredients in the Nutribullet and blend until smooth, about 20 seconds.

This recipe is packed with phytochemicals and antioxidants that are great for the heart. The avocadoes are concentrated with monounsaturated fatty acids that have been proven to reduce the risk of heart disease, while blueberries contain high quality antioxidants that will help your body prevent the accumulation of "bad" cholesterol.

Heart health blast (233 calories per serving)

Servings: 1

Ingredients

½ cup broccoli sprouts

½ inch ginger

¼ avocado

1 ½ cups coconut water

1 cup spinach

1 stalk celery

1 green apple, cored

1 pinch cayenne pepper

Directions

Combine all the ingredients in your NutriBullet, and process until smooth, about 20 seconds.

Leafy greens are filled with nitrates that help promote vascular health. They can help reduce your risk of having a stroke and heart attack. Avocadoes, on the other hand, are packed with healthy monounsaturated fats that are very helpful in maintaining healthy cholesterol levels.

Carrot fig blast (294 calories per serving)

Servings: 1

Ingredients

1 tablespoon hemp seeds

1 carrot

1 teaspoon cacao

1 cup spinach

½ banana

2 figs

1 ½ cups almond milk

Directions

Put all the ingredients in your Nutribullet and blend until smooth, about thirty seconds.

The figs in this recipe have been proven to counter high blood pressure, in addition to providing a sweet, delicate flavor. Carrots, on the other hand, are known for reducing the risk of cardiovascular disease.

Blueberry heaven Smoothie (446 calories per serving)

Servings: 1

Ingredients

¼ avocado

1 tablespoon hemp seeds

1 ½ cups coconut milk

1 cup spinach

1 tablespoon almond butter

1 cup blueberries

Directions

Combine all the ingredients in your NutriBullet, and process until smooth, about forty five seconds.

This heart healthy recipe is loaded with healthy fats that can help strengthen your bones, reduce your risk of vision problems related to age, and even prevent the development of cancer due to their folate content. Hemp seeds, on the other hand, can improve your immune function and help you maintain healthy cholesterol levels.

Heart healthy omega mix (205 calories per serving)

Servings: 1

Ingredients

½ avocado

1 tablespoon flax seeds

1 ½ cups arugula

1 plum

1 ½ cups water

Directions

Combine all the ingredients in your Nutribullet and process until smooth, about thirty seconds.

This recipe is the perfect blend of cholesterol fighting fiber and omega 3 fatty acids.

Greens oats and hemp seeds smoothie

Servings: 1

Ingredients

1 handful spinach

1/3 cup oats

1 tablespoon flax seeds

1 cup blackberries

1 cup almond milk

1 handful kale

1 cup peaches

1 tablespoon hemp seeds

2 tablespoons protein powder

2/3 cup coconut water

Directions

Put all ingredients in your Nutribullet and process until smooth, about thirty seconds.

Vegan peach oat blast (362 calories per serving)

Servings: 1

Ingredients

1 peach

1 tablespoon chia seeds

½ cup fresh orange juice

1 cup spinach

½ banana

¼ cup oats

1 cup almond milk

Directions

Combine all the ingredients in your Nutribullet and extract until smooth, about thirty seconds. Enjoy!

Oats are packed with heart healthy nutrients, as well as fiber to keep you full and satisfied for a long time.

Berry beet blast (233 calories per serving)

Servings: 1

Ingredients

1 cup strawberries

½ teaspoon ginger

2 cups coconut water

2/3 beet

1 teaspoon turmeric

1 orange

Directions

Combine all the ingredients in your Nutribullet and process for thirty seconds, or until smooth. Enjoy!

Raspberry blast (319 calories per serving)

Servings: 1

Ingredients

1 cup raspberries

3 slices cucumbers

½ teaspoon cinnamon

½ cup water

1 cup spinach

½ banana

1 tablespoon coconut oil

1 cup coconut milk

Directions

Blend all the ingredients in your NutriBullet for thirty seconds, or until smooth. Enjoy!

Raspberries are concentrated with fiber, manganese, vitamin C, and a variety of antioxidants such as resveratrol, flavanols, and anthocyanins, which will help promote your overall health and wellbeing. Adding cinnamon can also help balance your blood sugar levels.

Kiwi Guava and coconut smoothie (138 calories per serving)

Servings: 1

Ingredients

1 medium guava, sliced

¼ cup crushed ice

1 medium kiwi fruit, sliced

2/3 cup coconut water

Directions

Combine the crushed ice, coconut water, guava, and kiwi fruit in the NutriBullet, and process until smooth. Serve garnished with a piece of kiwi fruit, if desired.

Avocado cucumber and celery smoothie (105 calories per serving)

Servings: 1

Ingredients

½ medium cucumber, sliced

2 tablespoons of lime juice

1/8 medium avocado, sliced

1 diced celery stalk

1 teaspoon of agave nectar

Water to max line

Directions

Combine the agave nectar, lime juice, celery, cucumber, and avocado in the NutriBullet. Add water up to the max fill line, and process until smooth. Serve in a glass and garnish with a piece of lime or cucumber, if so desired.

Watercress cucumber celery and pineapple smoothie (88 calories per serving)

Servings: 1

Ingredients

1 medium celery stalk, diced

½ cup pineapple chunks

½ cup watercress, shredded

½ medium cucumber, sliced

Water to max line

Directions

Combine the pineapple, cucumber, celery, and watercress in your NutriBullet, and add water to the max fill line. Process until smooth, and then serve in a glass. Garnish with a piece of pineapple or cucumber, if so desired.

Strawberry kefir smoothie

Servings: 1

Ingredients

½ cup organic coconut milk

½ cup frozen organic strawberries

1 pinch of ground cinnamon

½ cup plain, non-fat Greek kefir

½ cup fresh organic strawberries

1 scoop protein powder or 2 raw eggs

1 teaspoon of raw honey or stevia to taste

Directions

Combine all the ingredients in the NutriBullet, and process until smooth.

Super red blast (233 calories per serving)

Servings: 1

Ingredients

1 carrot

1 cup strawberries

½ apple

1 small beet

1 inch ginger

1 tablespoon super food beauty boost

Water to max line

Directions

Combine all the ingredients in your NutriBullet, and process until smooth, about thirty seconds.

Apple a day smoothie

Servings: 1

Ingredients

½ avocado

7 walnuts

½ cup spinach

1 apple

½ teaspoon cinnamon

Almond milk to max line

Directions

Combine the ingredients in your NutriBullet and then process until smooth.

Apples are packed with bioflavanoid antioxidants that have been shown to counter the wear and tear associated with aging, prevent the development of cancer, and ease inflammation.

Lime kiwi blast (233 calories per serving)

Servings: 1

Ingredients

1 kiwi

¼ lime

Ice cubes

1 cup spinach

1 medium pear

1 teaspoon honey

Water to max line

Directions

Combine all the ingredients in your NutriBullet, and process until smooth.

This recipe includes kiwi fruit, which is loaded with vitamin C, vitamin E, folic acid, and antioxidants, will of which work together to improve your immune system and prevent heart disease. Lime, on the other hand, is great for your skin and digestion, as well as for providing a tasty flavor.

Conclusion

Thank you again for reading this book!

I hope this book was able to help you know several Nutribullet smoothie recipes that you can make. The next step is to try out these recipes and you will not regret it.

Finally, if you enjoyed this book, would you be kind enough to leave a review for this book on Amazon?

Thank you and good luck!

CPSIA information can be obtained
at www.ICGtesting.com
Printed in the USA
BVHW041056150521
607436BV00003B/562